PLAY GUITAR WITH
The best of U2

MW00999427

Published by
Wise Publications
8/9 Frith Street, London W1D 3JB, England

Exclusive Distributors:
Music Sales Limited
Distribution Centre, Newmarket Road, Bury St Edmunds, Suffolk IP33 3YB
Music Sales Pty Limited
120 Rothschild Avenue, Rosebery, NSW 2018, Australia

Compiled by Nick Crispin
Music arranged by Arthur Dick
Music processed by Paul Ewers Music Design
Project Editor: Tom Fleming
Printed in the United Kingdom

CD recorded, mixed and mastered by Jonas Persson
All guitars by Arthur Dick
Bass by Paul Townsend
Drums by Brett Morgan
Strings on 'All I Want Is You' by Rick Cardinali
Harmonica on 'Desire' by Stuart Constable

www.musicsales.com

Wise Publications
part of The Music Sales Group
London/New York/Paris/Sydney/Copenhagen/Berlin/Madrid/Tokyo

All I Want Is You

Words & Music by U2

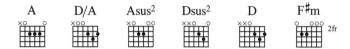

Tune all guitars down a semitone

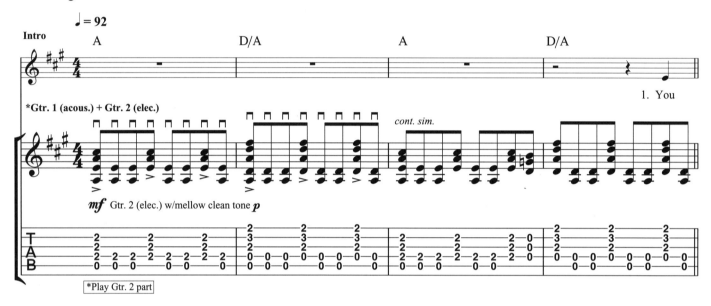

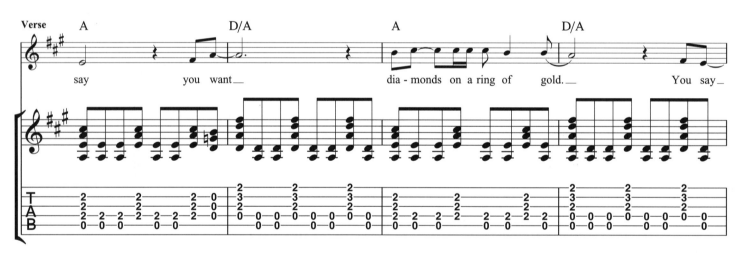

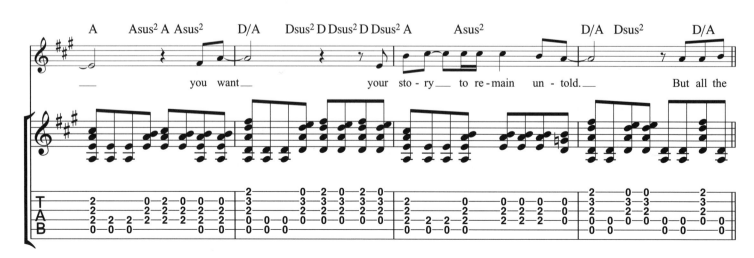

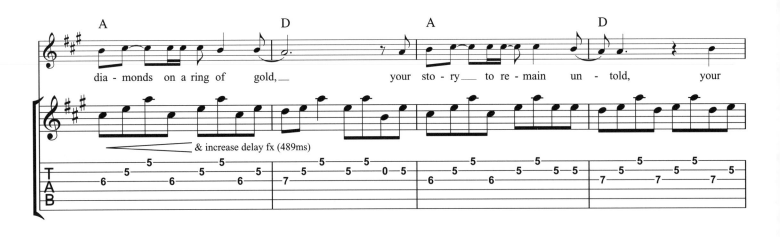

diamonds on a ring of gold, your story to remain untold, your

& increase delay fx (489ms)

love not to grow cold. All the promises we break from the

Chorus

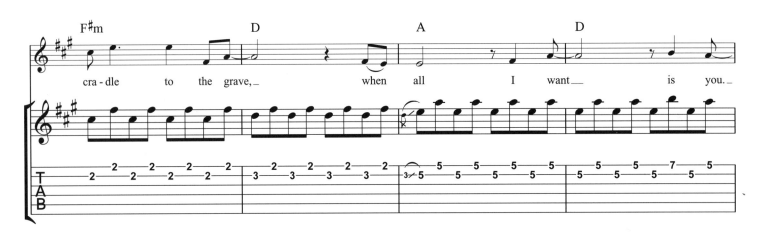

cradle to the grave, when all I want is you.

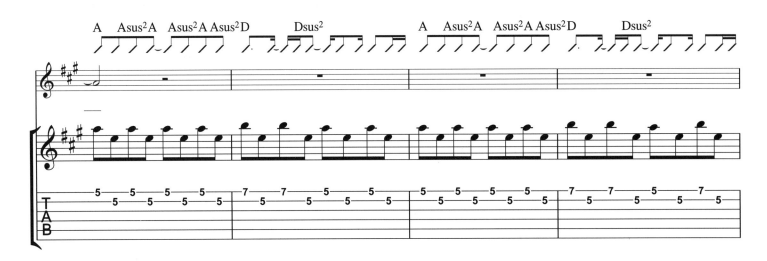

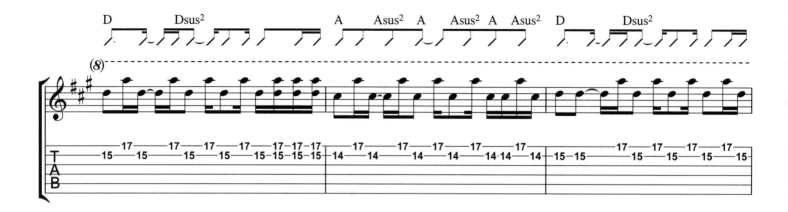

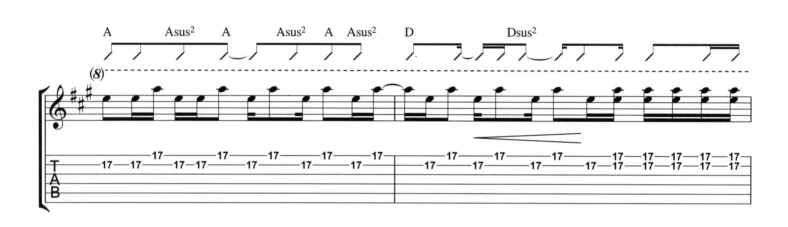

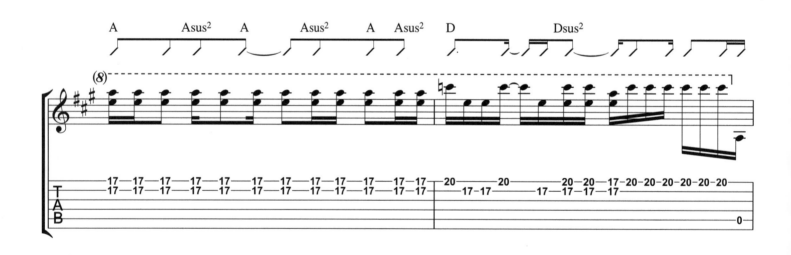

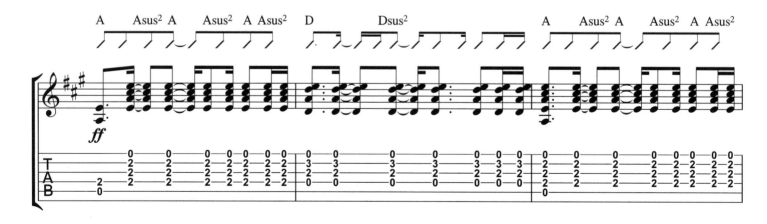

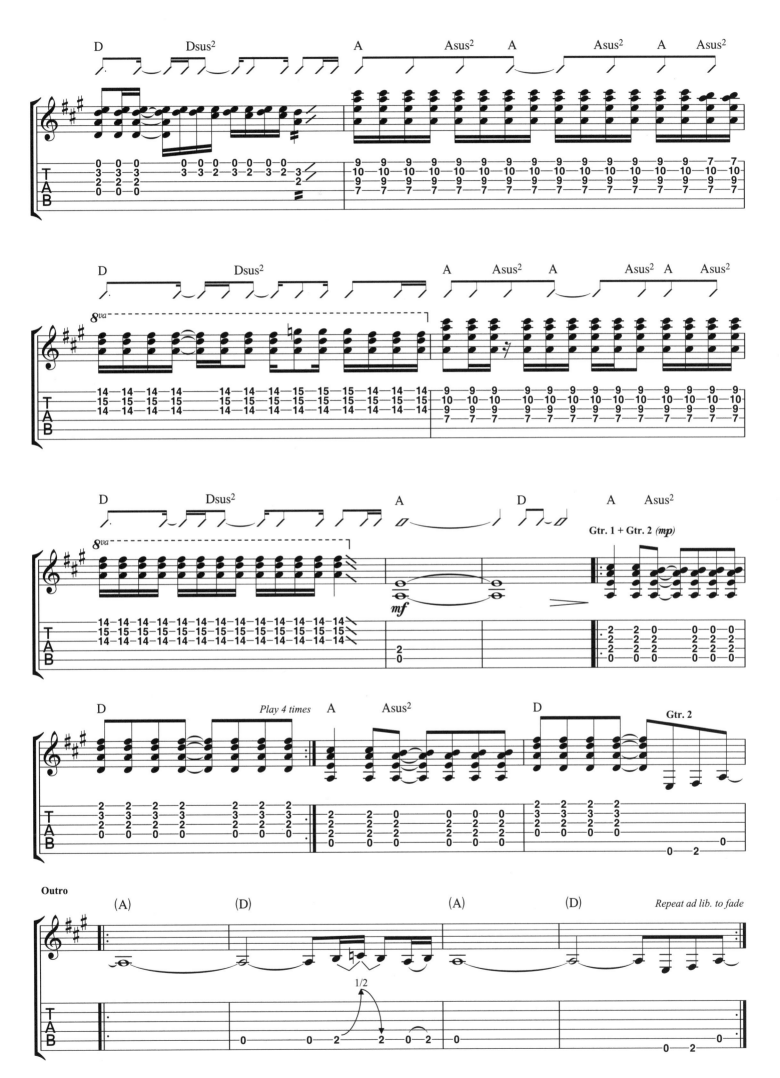

Beautiful Day

Words by Bono. Music by U2

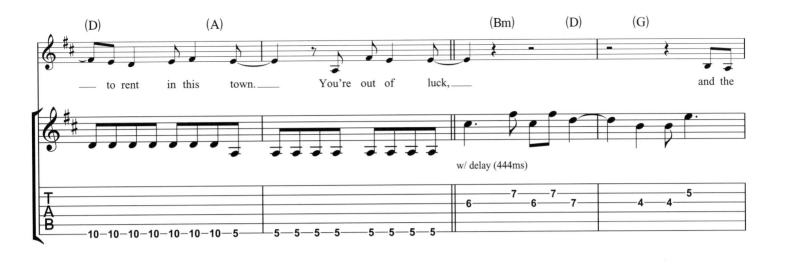

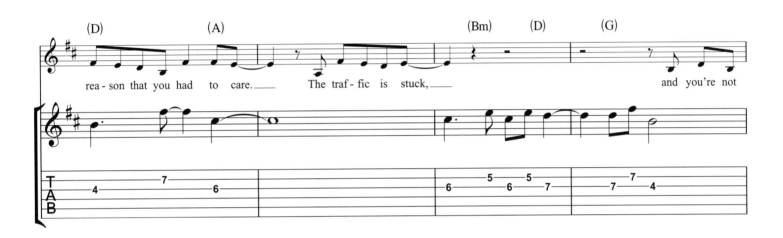

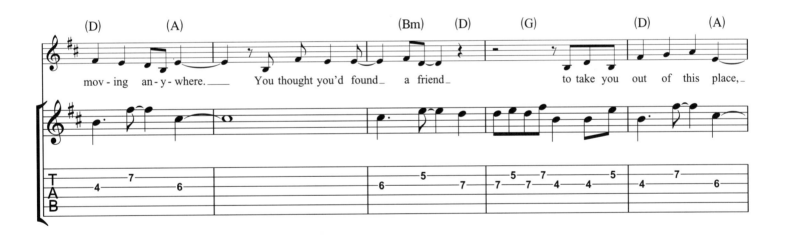

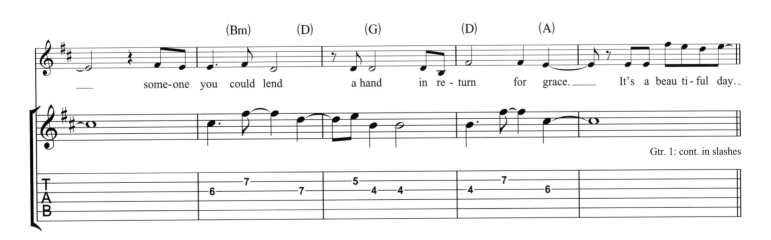

Elevation

Words by Bono. Music by U2

ex - ca - va - tion. I and I in the sky,____ you make me feel like I can
ex - ca - va - tion. I and I in the sky,____ you make me feel like I can

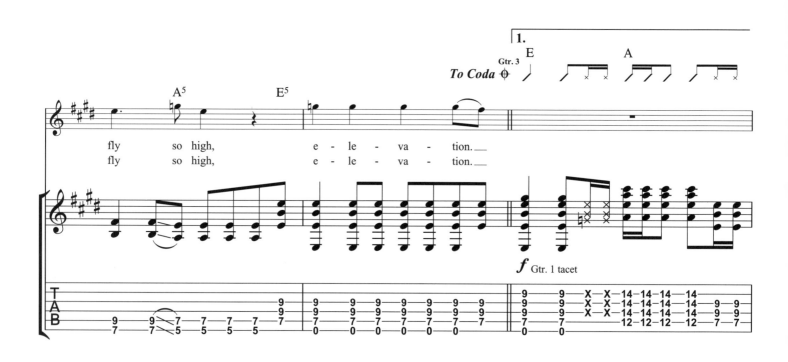

fly so high, e - le - va - tion.____
fly so high, e - le - va - tion.____

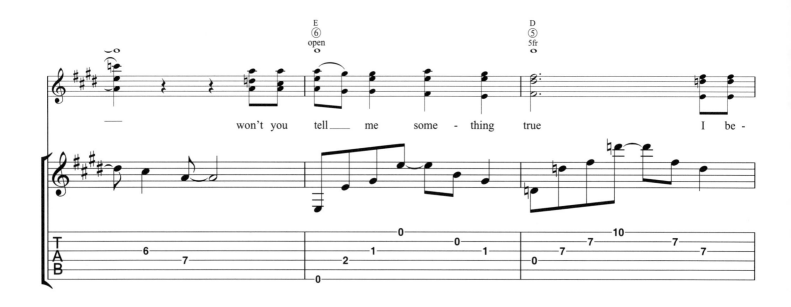

won't you   tell___ me   some - thing   true   I   be -

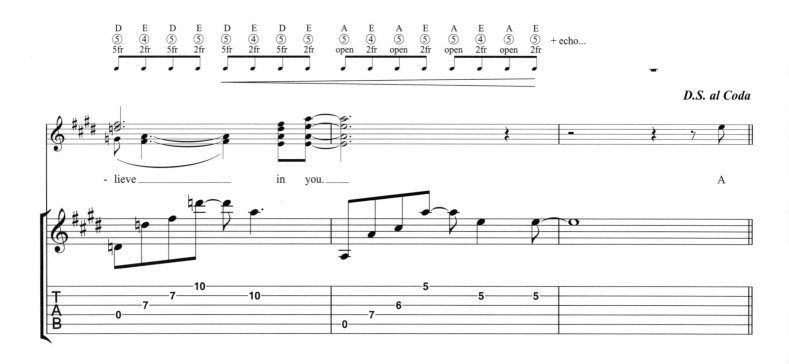

+ echo...

D.S. al Coda

- lieve _____   in   you. ___   A

Coda

N.C.

E - le - va - tion.   E - le - va - tion.

Gtr. 2+3

ff   w/dist + wah-wah

Even Better Than The Real Thing

Words & Music by U2

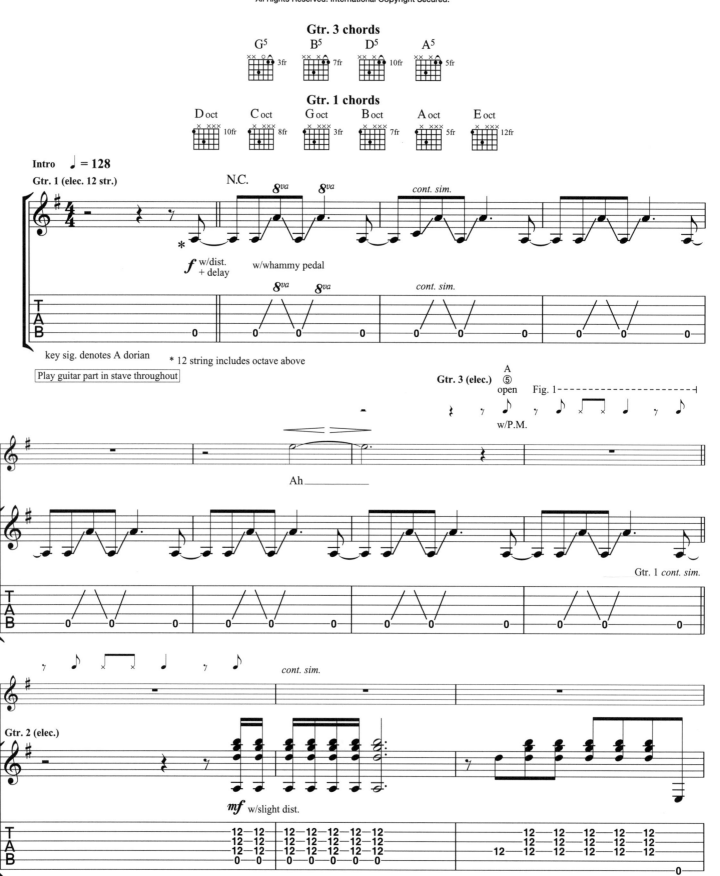

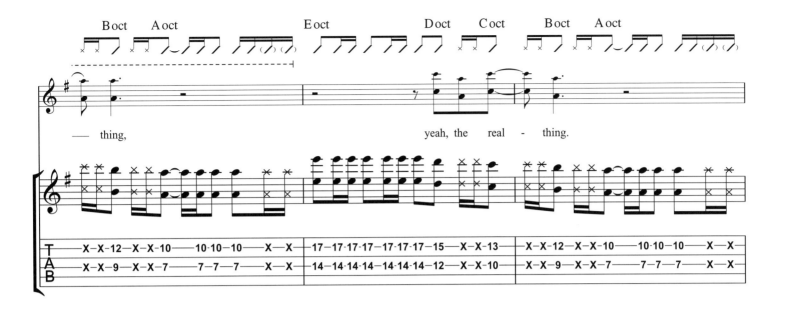

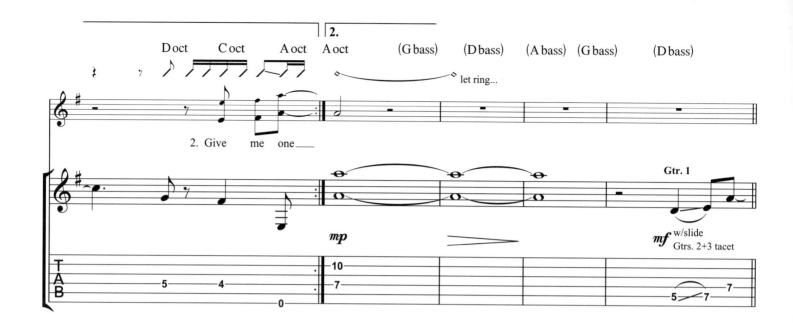

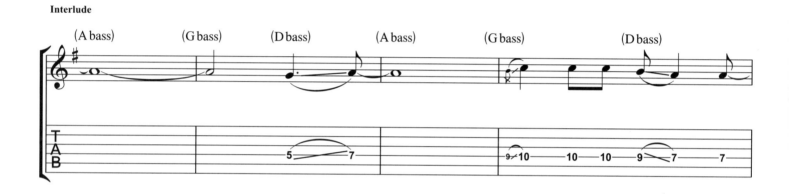

Interlude

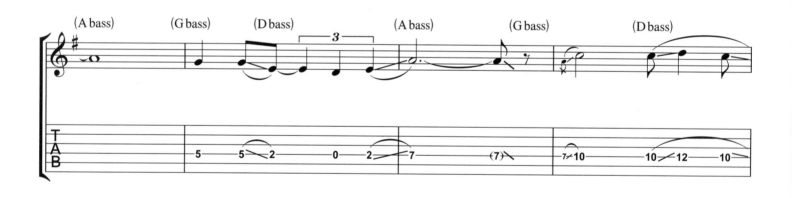

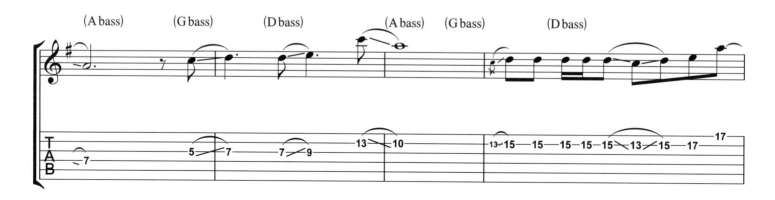

* sound higher 3rd string if using 12 string

Hold Me, Thrill Me, Kiss Me, Kill Me

Words & Music by U2

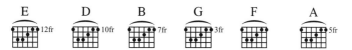

Tune guitars down a semitone

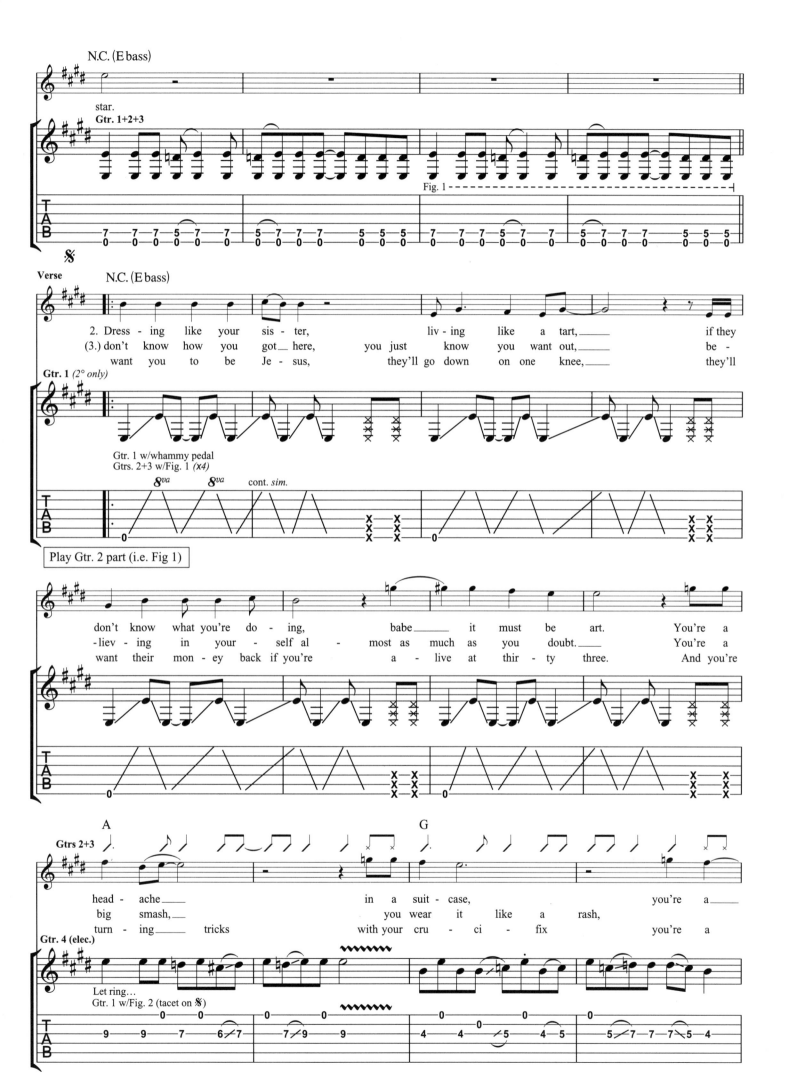

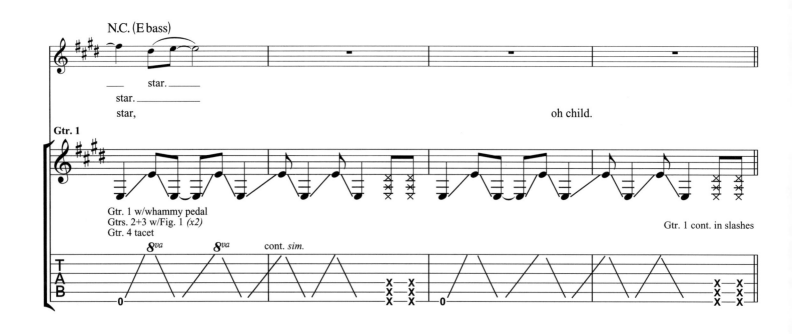

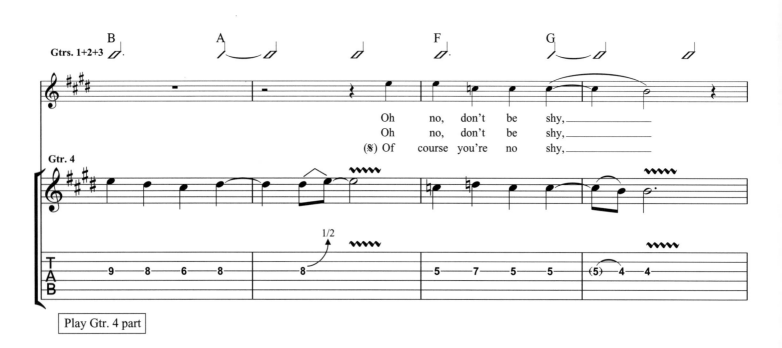

Play Gtr. 4 part

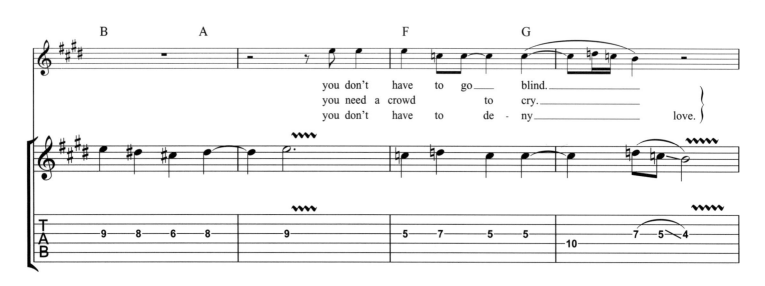

I Still Haven't Found What I'm Looking For

Words & Music by U2

Gtr. 3 chords

Gtrs. 5+6 chords

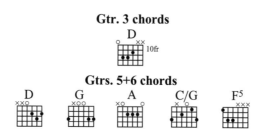

Tune all guitars down a semitone

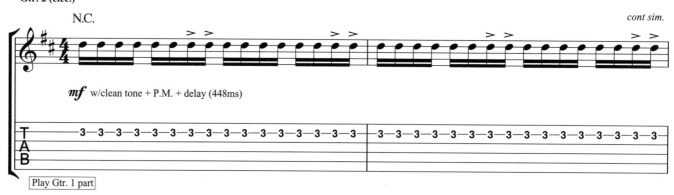

* slightly P.M. 4th string, let others ring

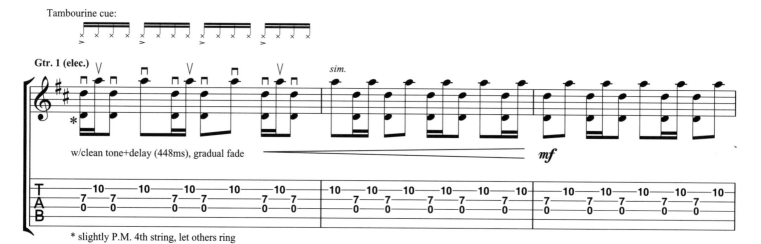

Gtr. 3 w/dist, 6th string tuned to D

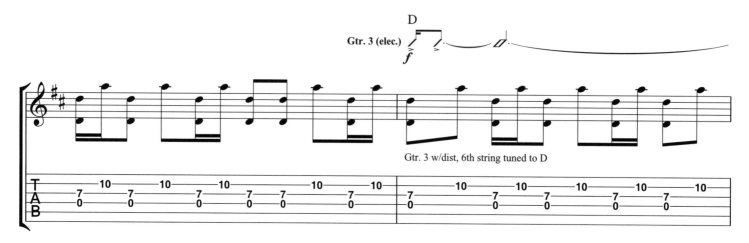

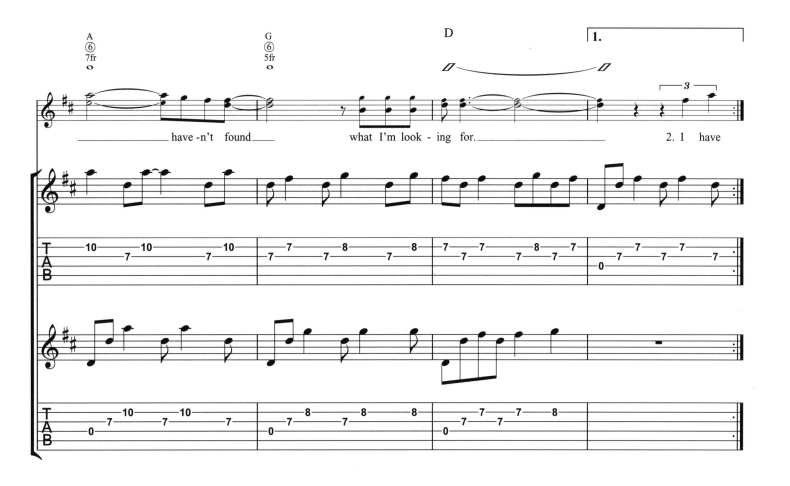

have -n't found what I'm look - ing for. 2. I have

Interlude

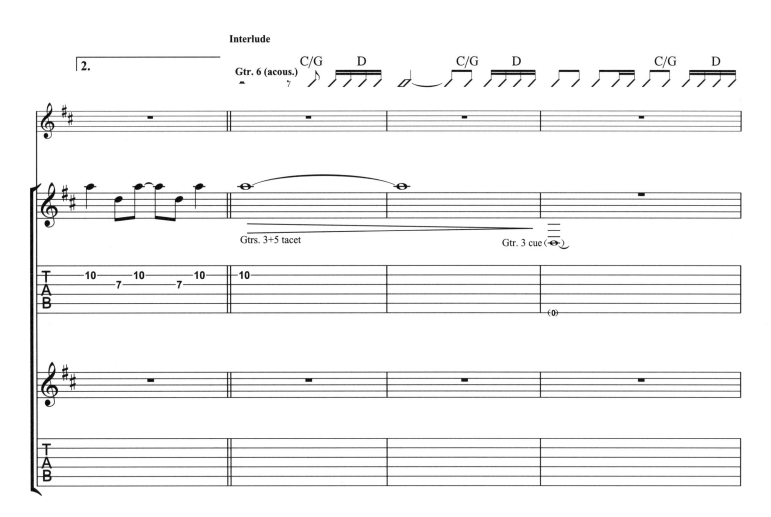

Gtr. 6 (acous.)

Gtrs. 3+5 tacet

Gtr. 3 cue

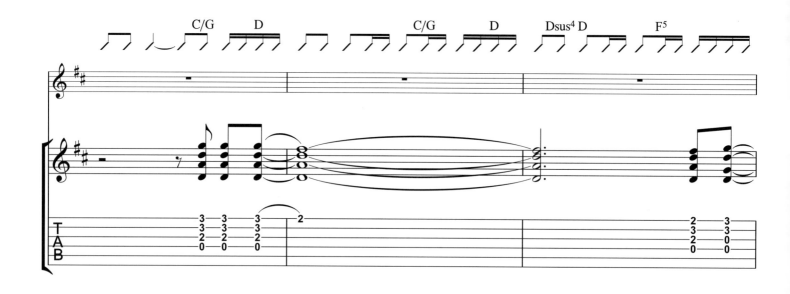

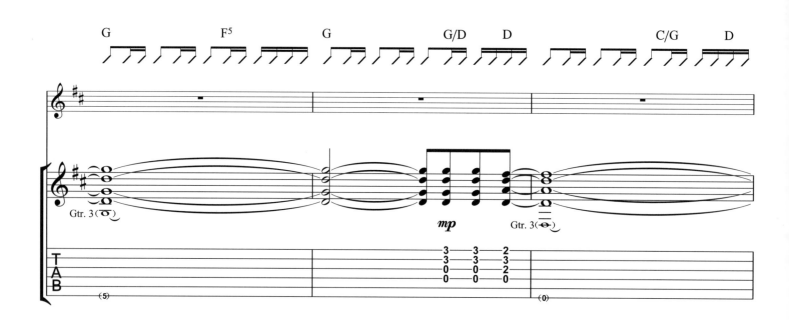

to one,___ bleed in - to one._____ But yes I'm still_____ run - nin'.___

You broke the bonds___ and you loosed the chains,___ car - ry the cross___ of my

___ shame of the ___ shame,_____ you know I be - lieve it._____

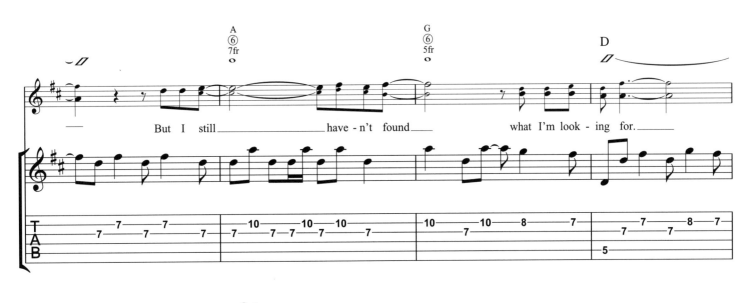

But I still _____ have-n't found _____ what I'm look-ing for.

cont. sim.

Outro

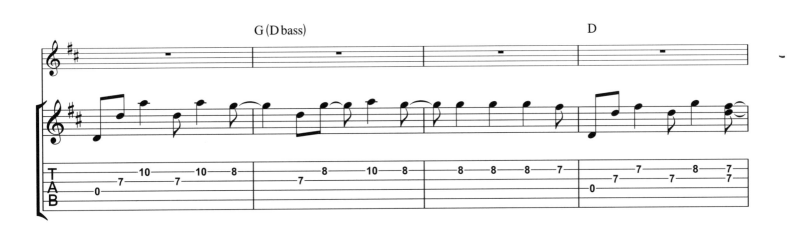

Repeat to fade

New Year's Day

Words & Music by U2

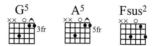

Tune all guitars down a semitone

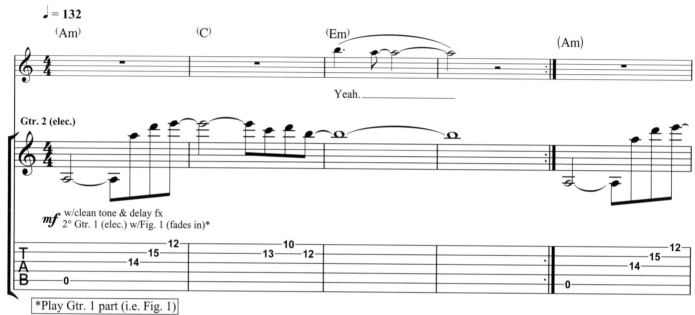

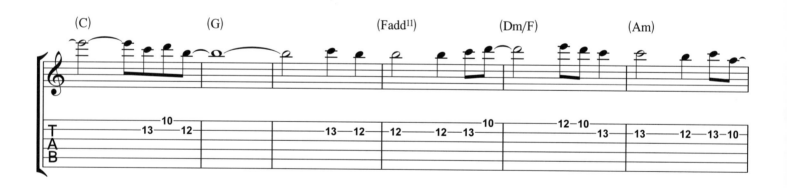

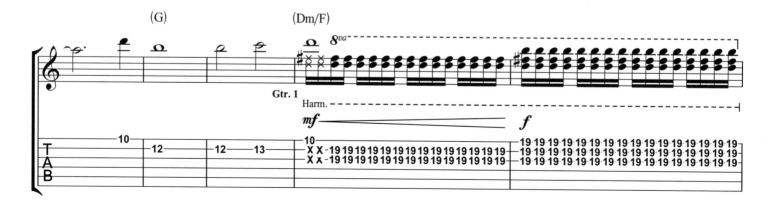

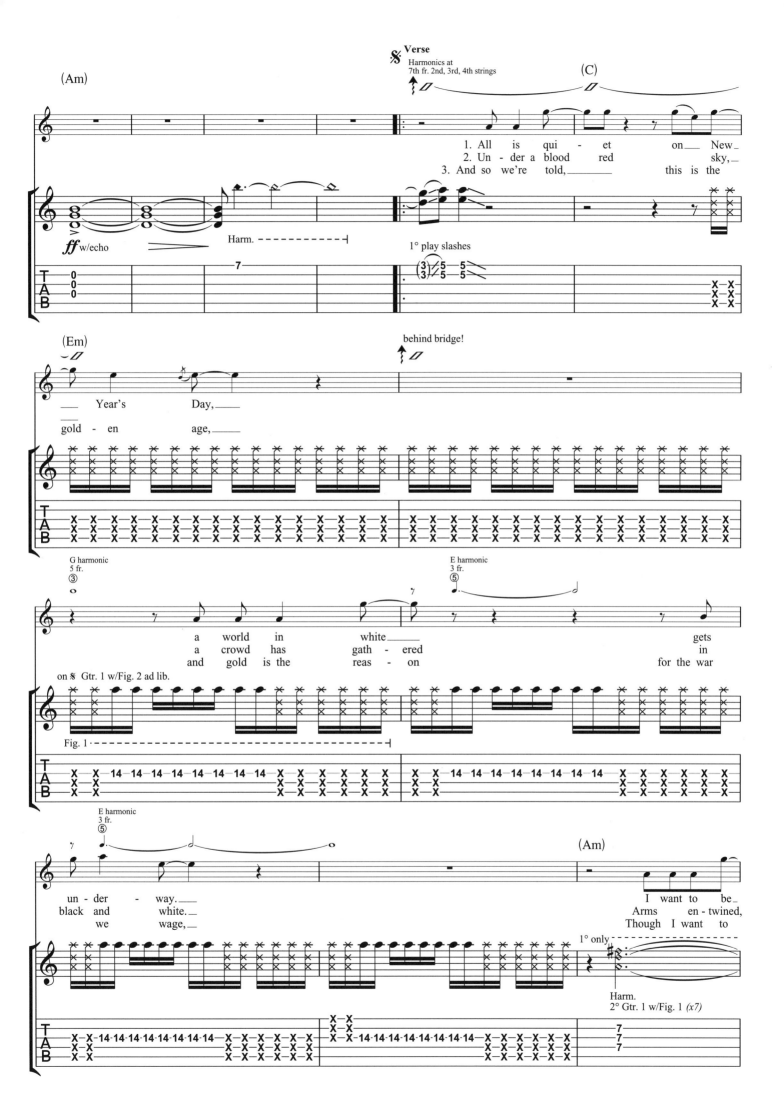

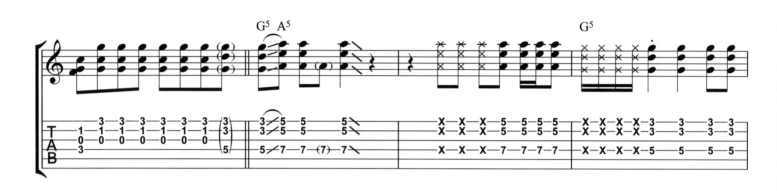

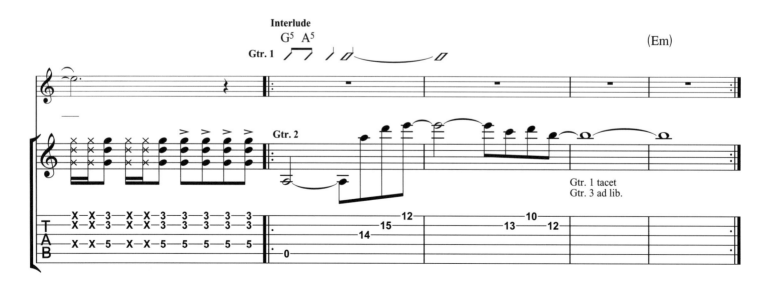

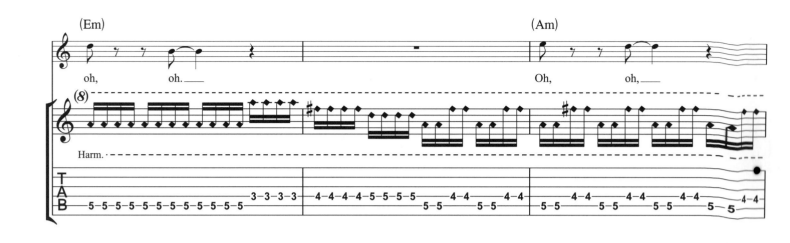

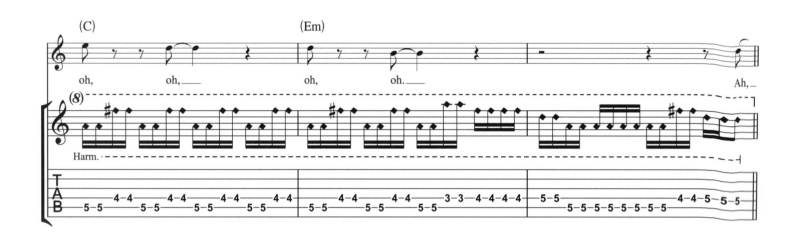

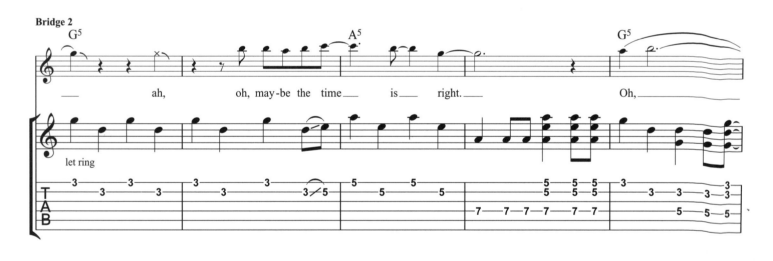

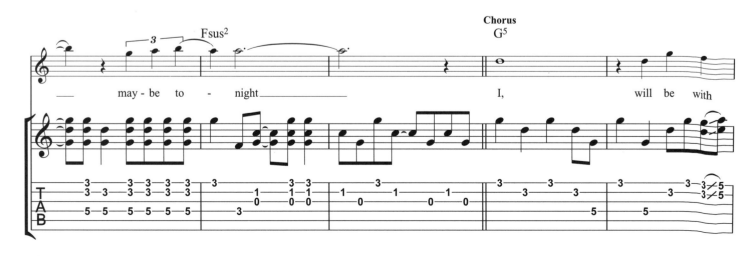

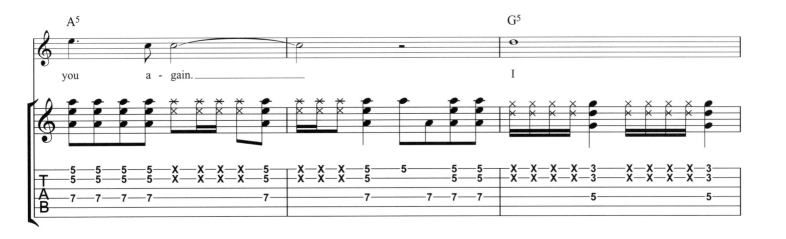

you   a - gain._____   I

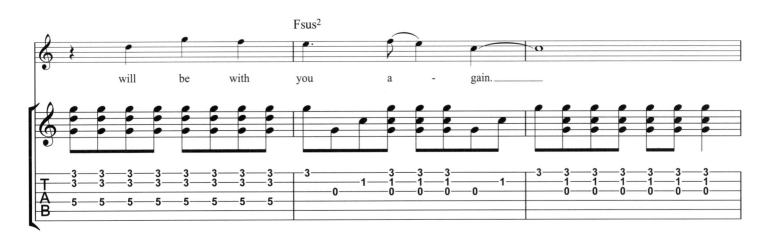

will   be   with   you   a - gain._____

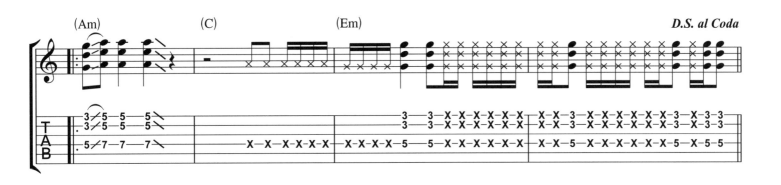

On___ New ___Year's Day.___

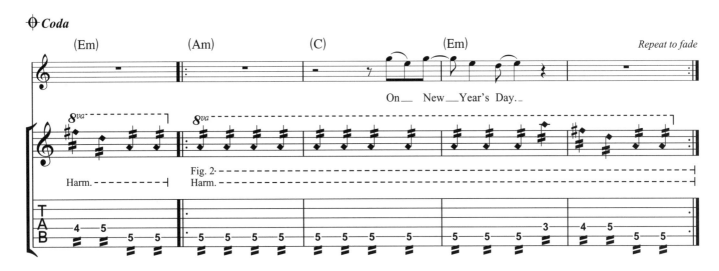

Desire

Words by Bono. Music by U2

57

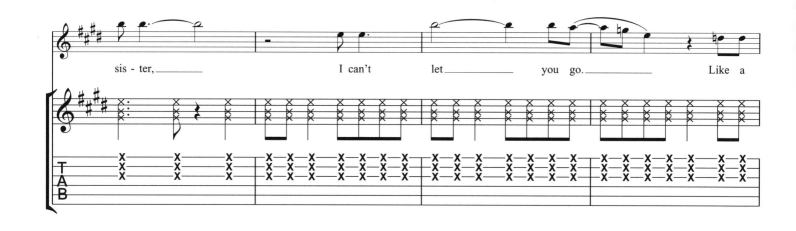

sis - ter,_____ I can't let_____ you go._____ Like a

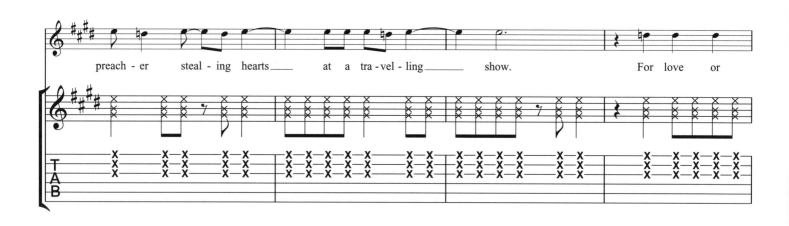

preach - er steal - ing hearts_____ at a tra - vel - ling_____ show. For love or

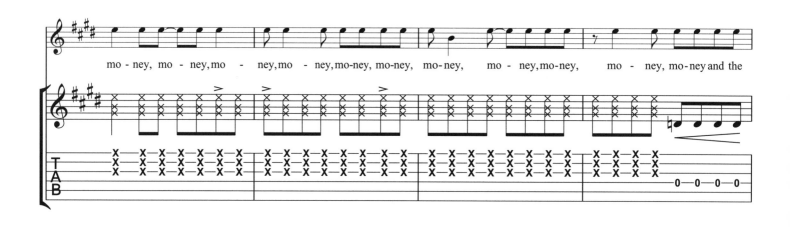

mo - ney, mo - ney, mo - ney, mo - ney, mo-ney, mo-ney, mo - ney, mo - ney, mo-ney, mo - ney, mo-ney and the

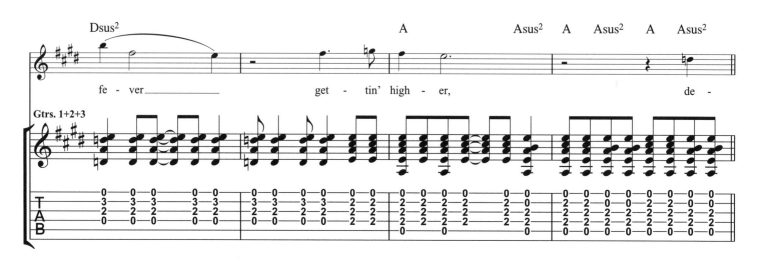

fe - ver_____ get - tin' high - er, de -

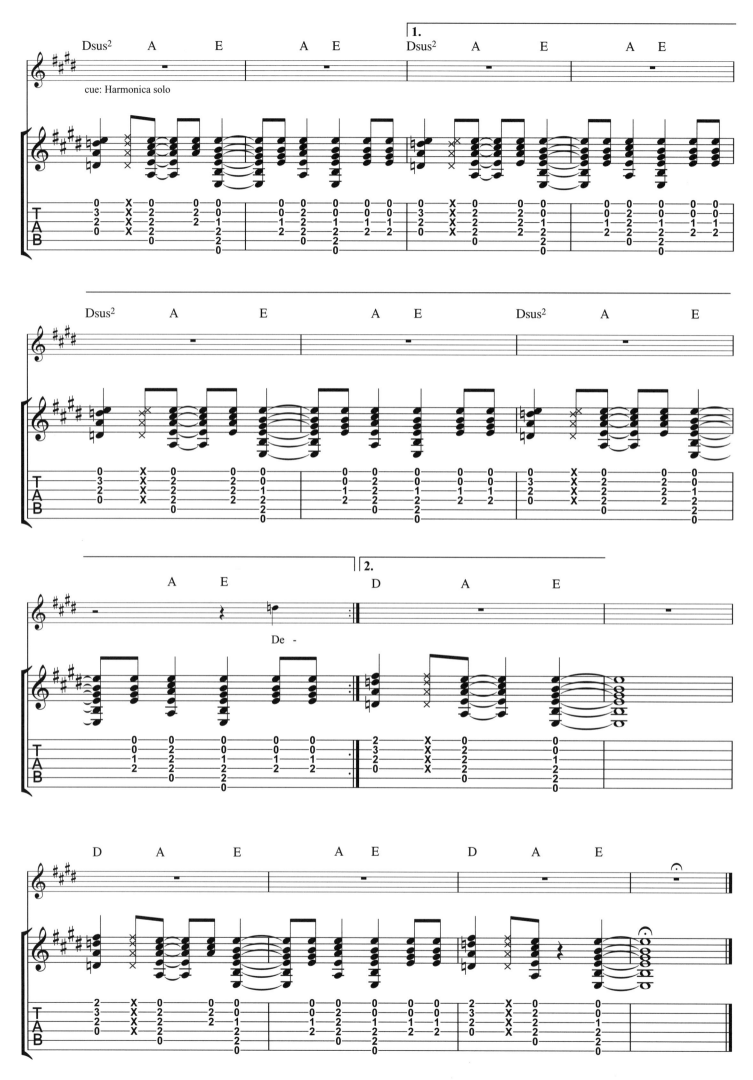

One

Words & Music by U2

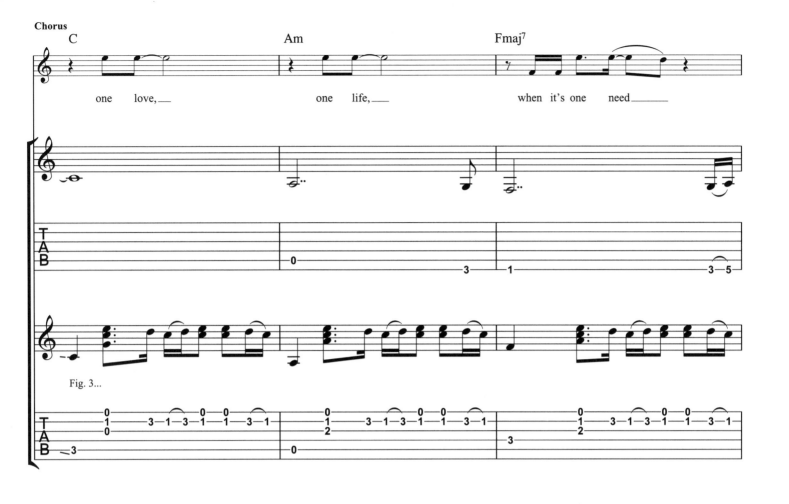

one love,___ one life,___ when it's one need_____

Fig. 3...

in the night. One love,___ we get_ to share_ it,___

...Fig. 3 ends Fig. 1 -

leaves you ba - by if you don't care_____ for it._____

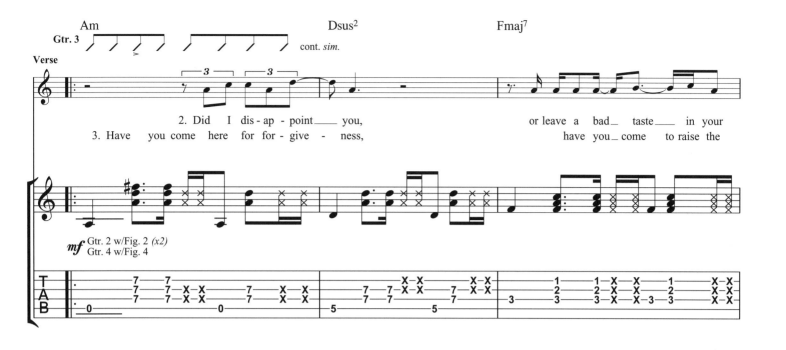

2. Did I dis - ap - point___ you,   or leave a bad_ taste___ in your
3. Have you come here for for - give - ness,   have you__ come   to raise the

mouth?   You act___ like you nev - er had love,___
dead?   Have you come here___ to play Je - sus,

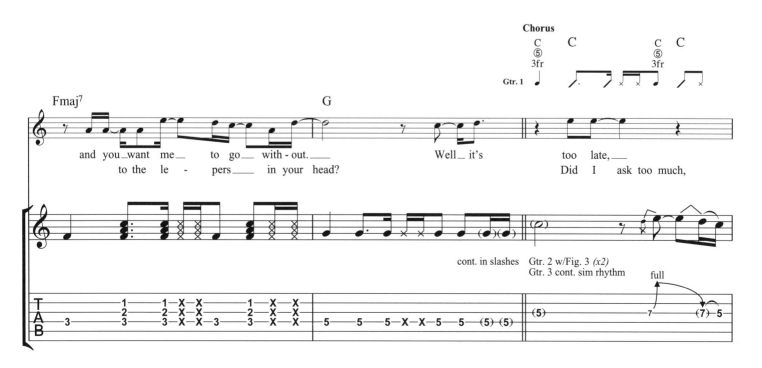

and you_want me___   to go   with - out.___   Well_ it's   too late,___
to the le - pers___   in your head?   Did I   ask too much,

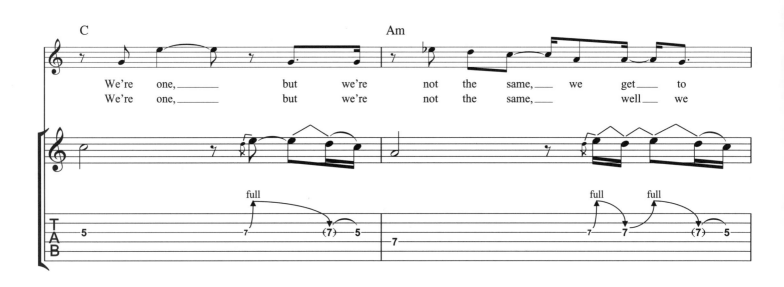

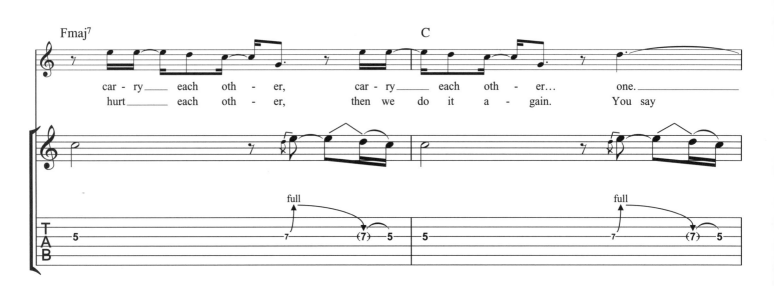

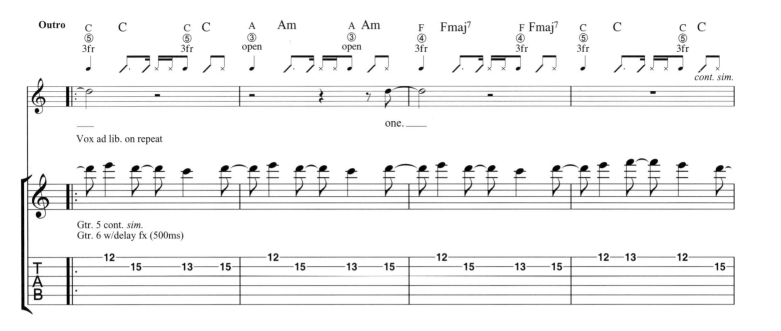

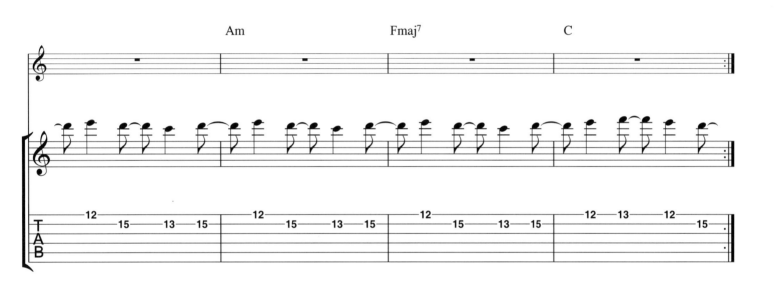

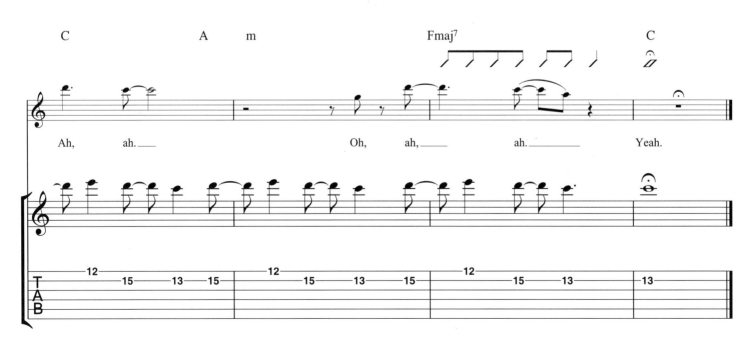

Pride (In The Name Of Love)

Words & Music by U2

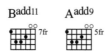

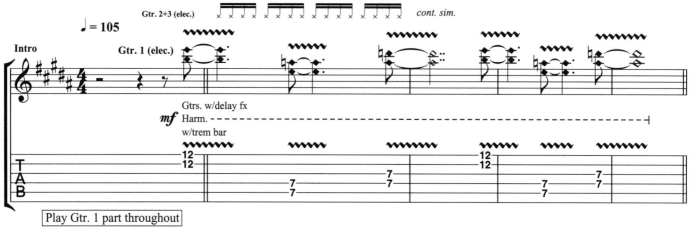

Play Gtr. 1 part throughout

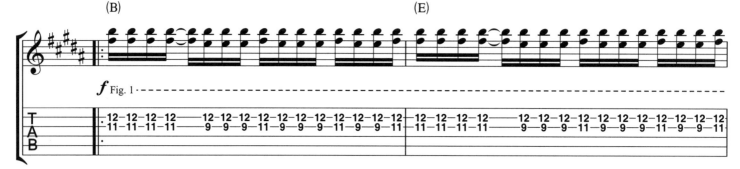

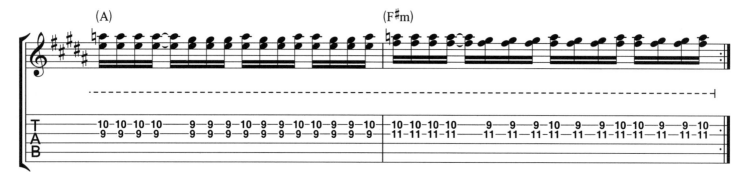

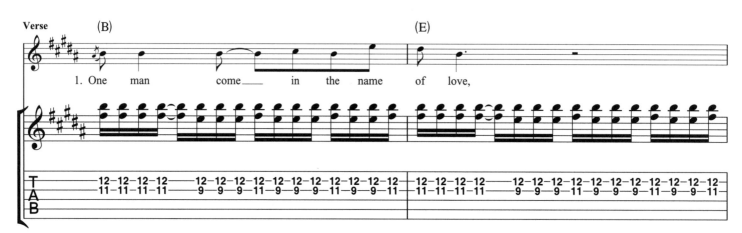

1. One man come in the name of love,

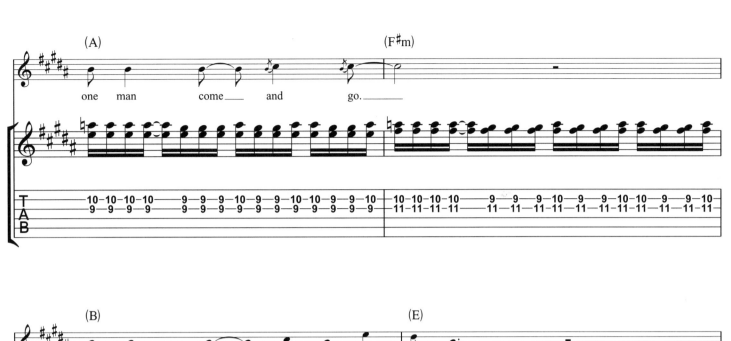

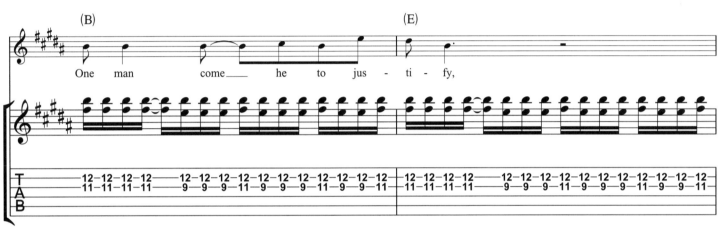

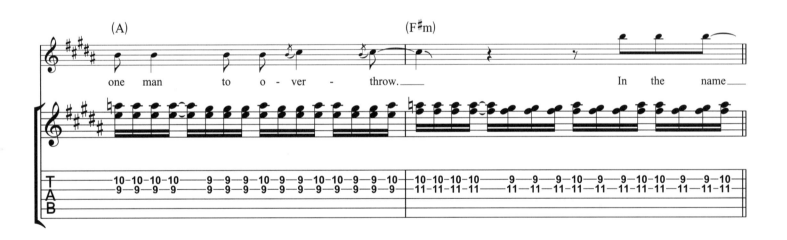

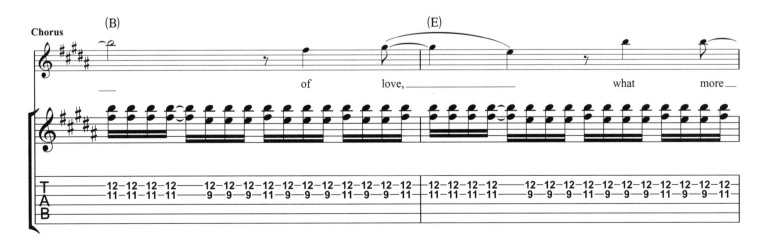

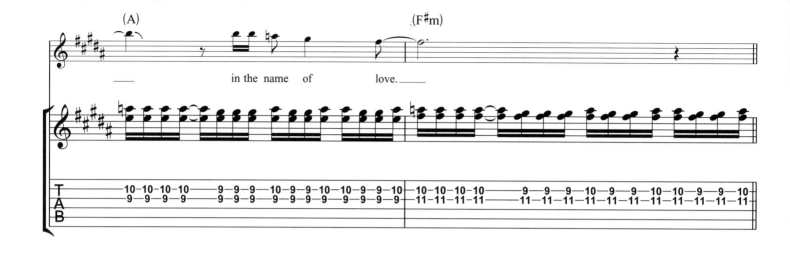

in the name of love.

Interlude

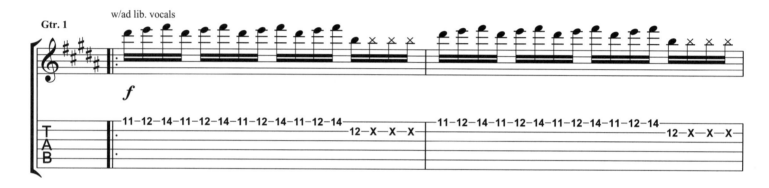

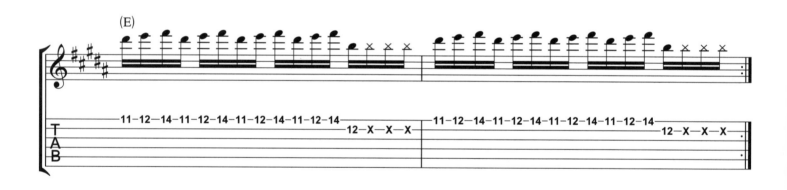

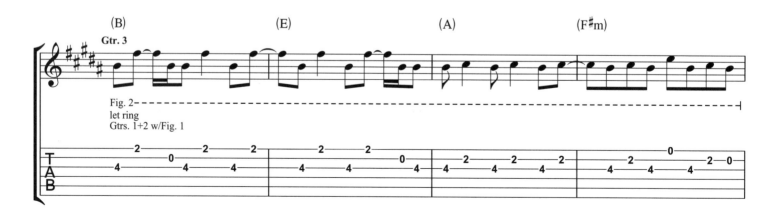

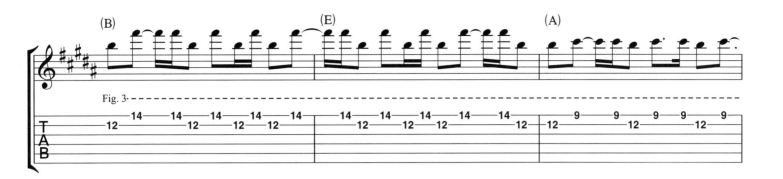

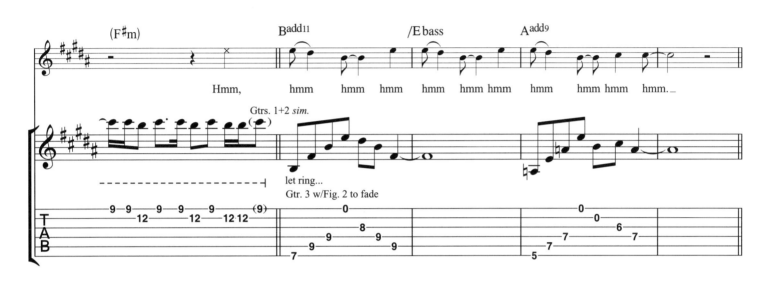

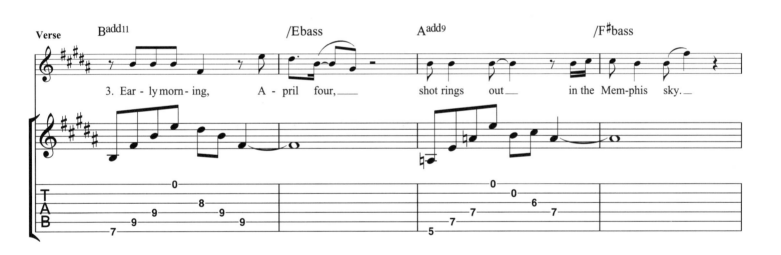

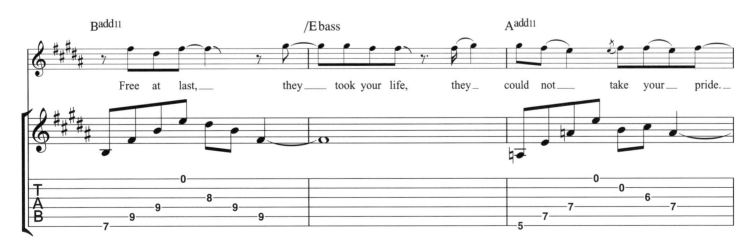

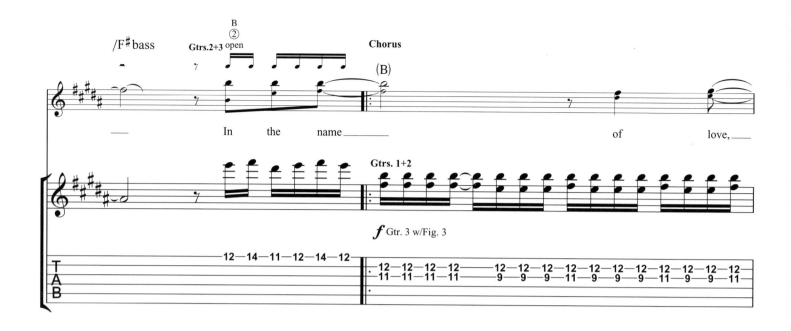

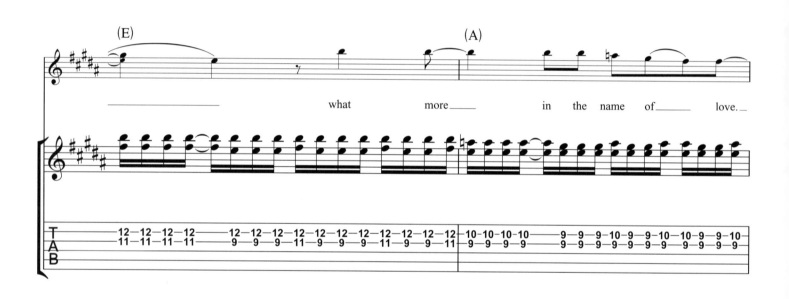

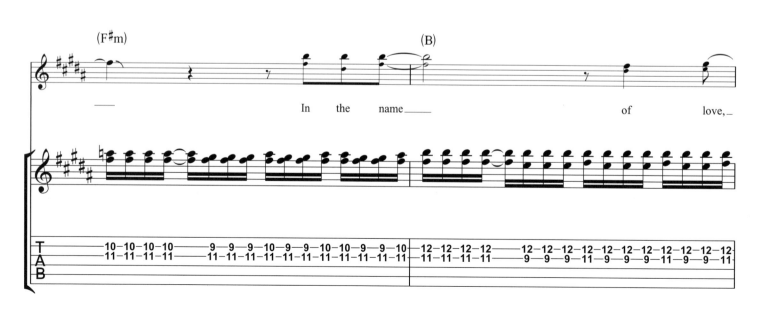

U2 - Sunday Bloody Sunday

```
Intr[4] Arpeggio[2]
V1    [2] "Can't believe the news today..." Arpeggio
PC    [2] "How Long..." Sustained Strums (D Em D Em7)
C1    [2] "Tonight..."   Anthem
V2    [4] "Broken bottle…" Anthem[1], Arpeggio[3]
Sun   [2] "Sunday" Arpeggio
B1    [4] Harmonics[2] Anthem[2]
V3    [4] "Battle's just begun" Anthem[1], Arpeggio[3]
Sun   [2] "Sunday" Arpeggio
PC    [2] "How long"  Sustained Strums
C2    [4] "Tonight" Anthem
Solo[4] 12-10
Wipe[4] "Wipe" Chunk[3]
Sun   [2] "Sunday" Chunk[2]
B     [4] Harmonics[4]
Solo[2] Fiddle solo, Anthem
V4    [8] "True we all are new" Anthem
```

U2 - Pride (In the name of Love)

```
Intr [2]
Theme[4]
V1    [4] "One Man…" Theme
C1    [4] "In the name" Theme
V2    [4] "One Man…" Chime Arpeggio
C2    [4] "In the name" Theme
S1    [4] 11-12-14
S2    [4]
      [2] "oooh" Chime Arpeggio
V3    [4] "Early Morning" Chime Arpeggio
C3    [8] "In the name" Theme
Outro[6] "oooh"
```

Led Zeppelin - Over the Hills and Far Away

Intro (Riff)
V1 "hey Lady" Riff > high chords
V2 "Many times" Chords
V3
B1 > Solo
V4 "Mello is a man"
V5 "Many is a word"

Knocking on Heavens Door

```
G/D/Am7   G/D/C(D)
```

Hotel California

```
Bm/F#    A/E   G/D    Em     F#
G/D(pinch) Em/Bm7(ascending)  G/D   Em     F#
```

Wish you were here
```
C/D  Am/G  D/C  Am/G
Em G Em G Em A Em A G
```


The Ocean
```
Riff
V1 "Singin in the Sunshine"
Riff
V2 "Singin to an Ocean"
Riff/Solo
V3 "Ooh yeah"
"Na Na"
V4 "Rounds Singin Songs"
Riff
Swing/Solo
```

Something (Beatles)
```
C Cmaj7
C7 F
D   G
Am Am(maj7)  b-string  10-13BR-10-11-12-13

A  (C#m)  F#m7
D  G  A
A  (C#m)  F#m7
D - G  A
```
I don't Know
i've got a feeling (Beatles)

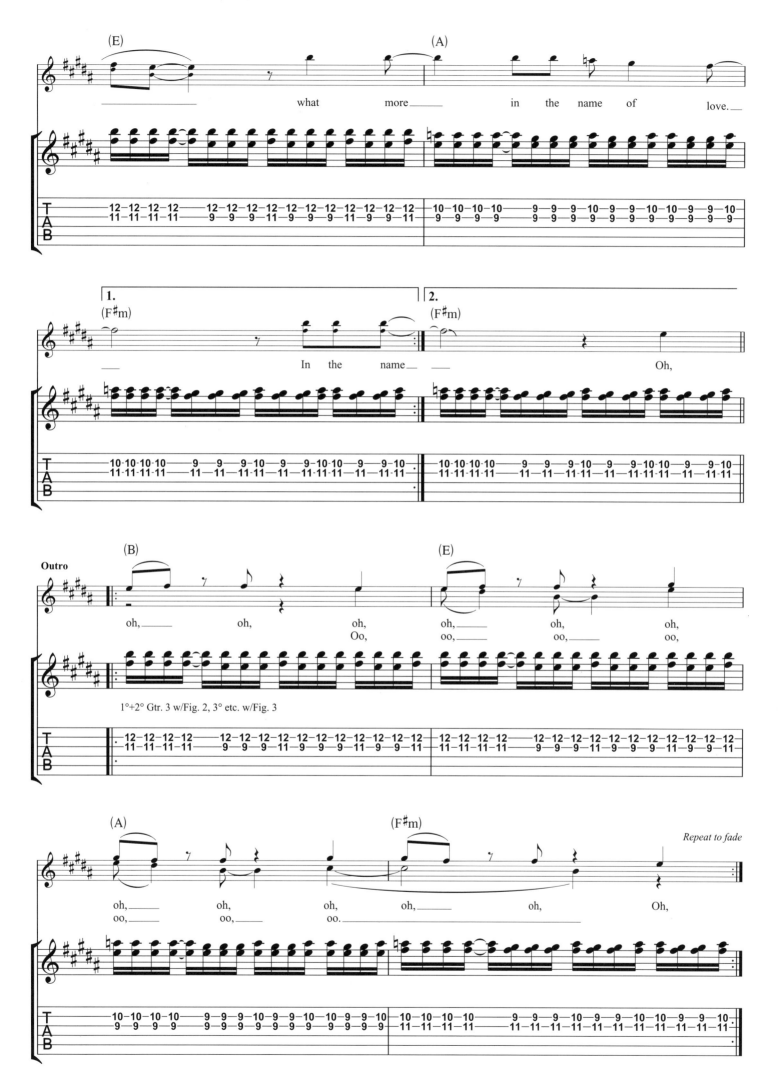

Sunday Bloody Sunday

Words & Music by U2

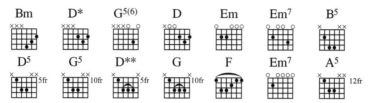

Tune guitars down a semitone

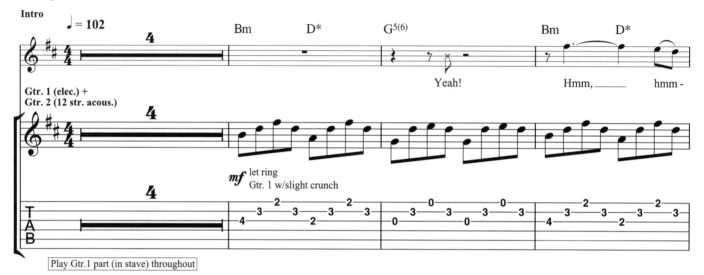

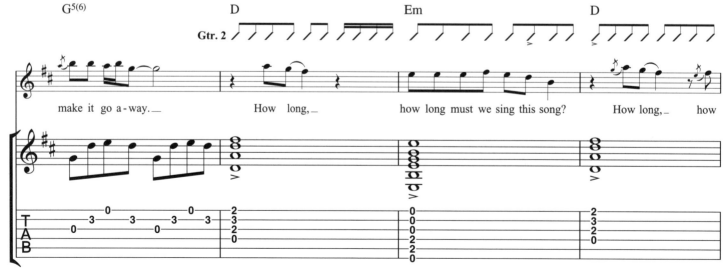

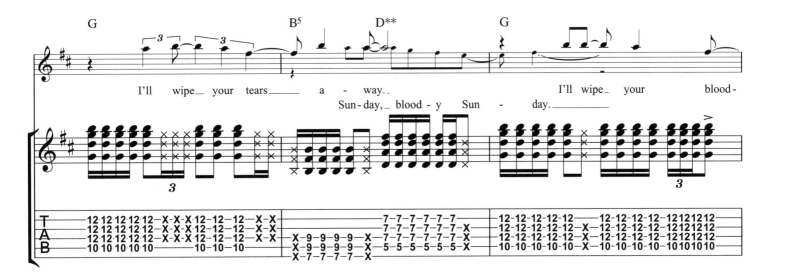

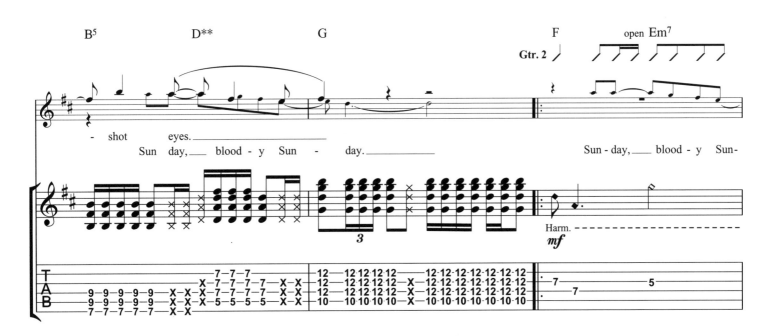

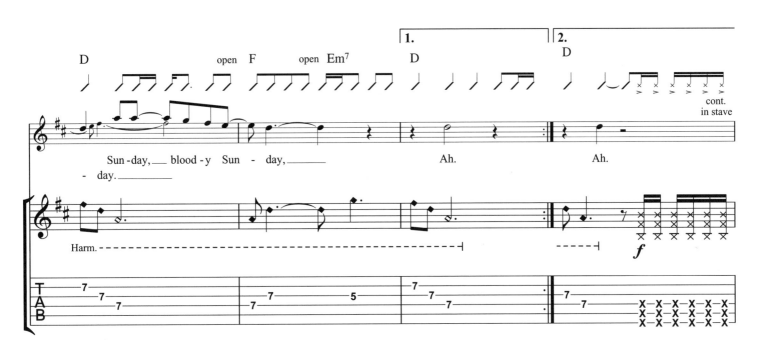

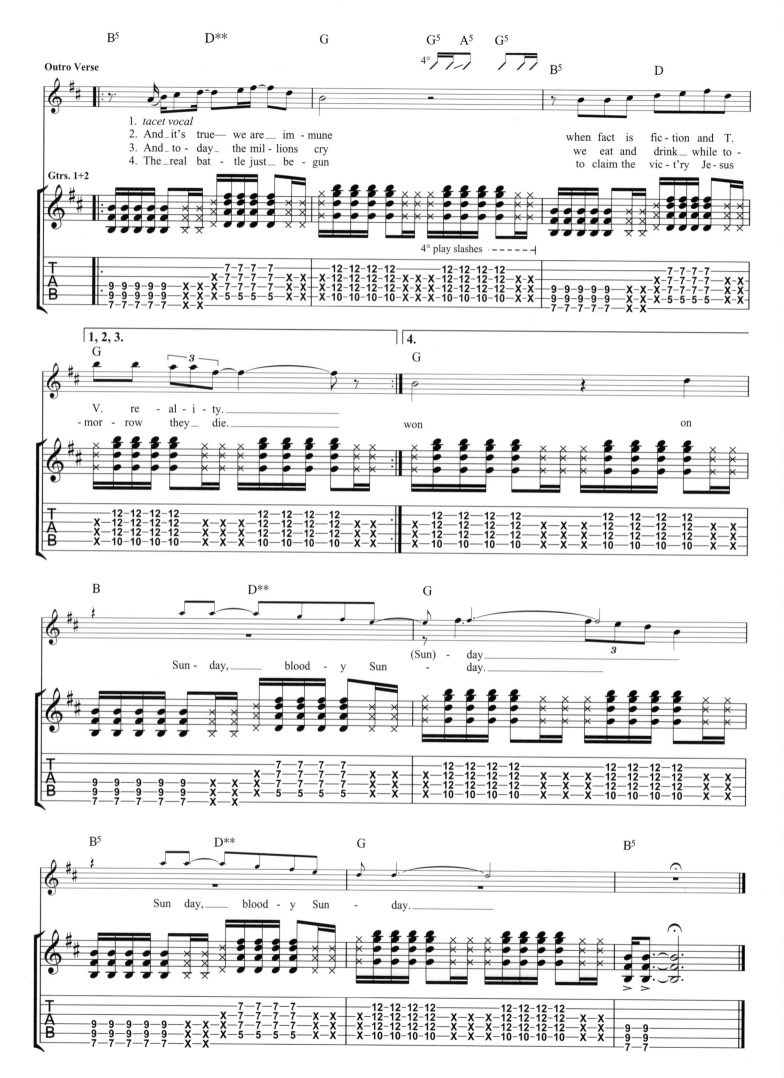

Where The Streets Have No Name

Words & Music by U2

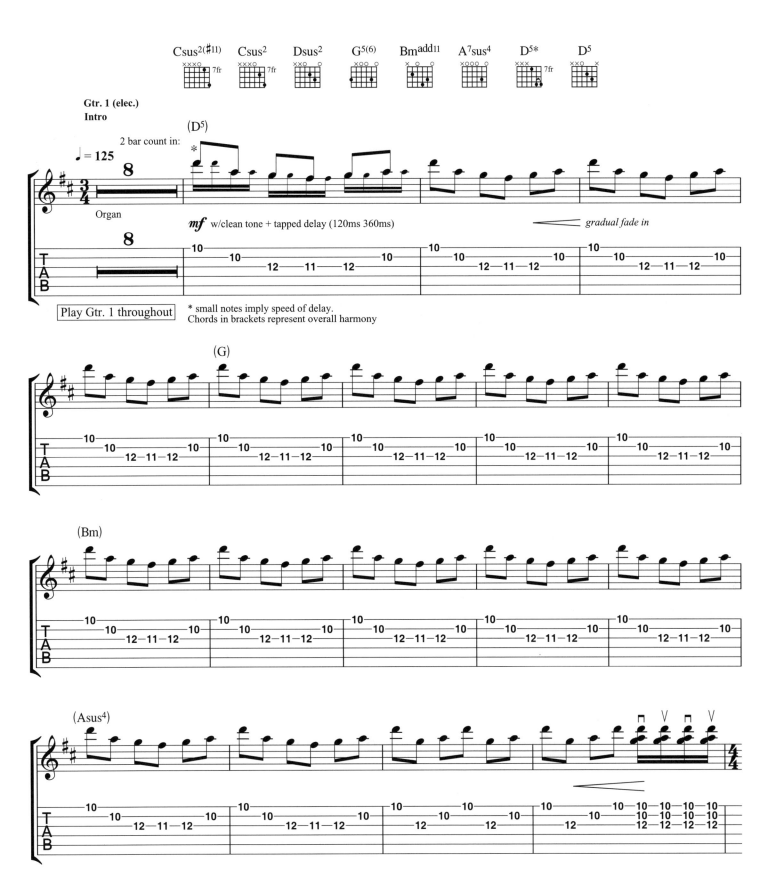

Play Gtr. 1 throughout

* small notes imply speed of delay.
Chords in brackets represent overall harmony

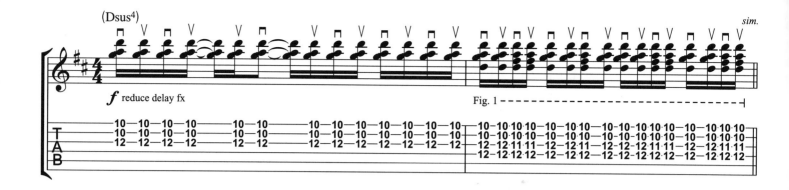

Gtrs. 1+2 (elec.)

* abbreviated notation - hold and strum shape moving 3rd string harmony as indicated (i.e. as Fig. 1)

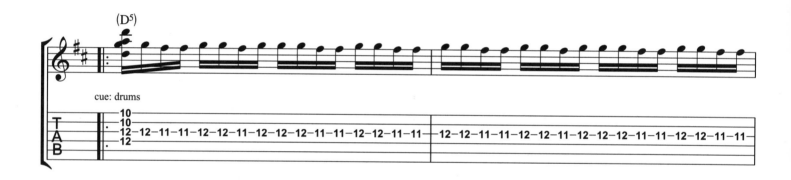

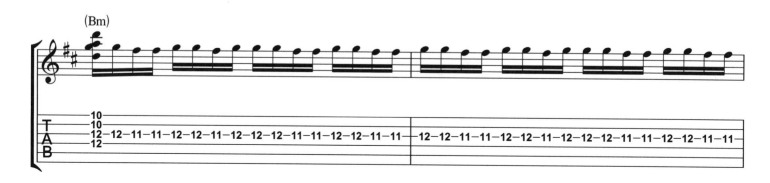

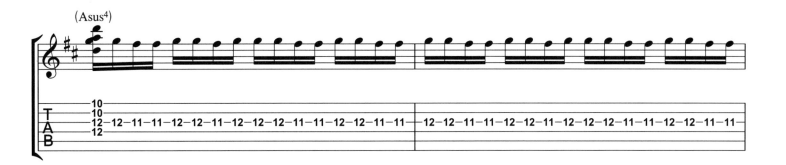

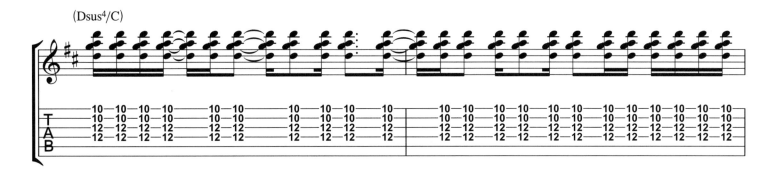

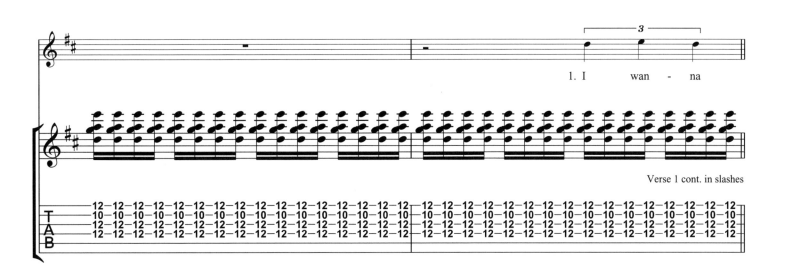

Verse 1 cont. in slashes

1. I wan - na

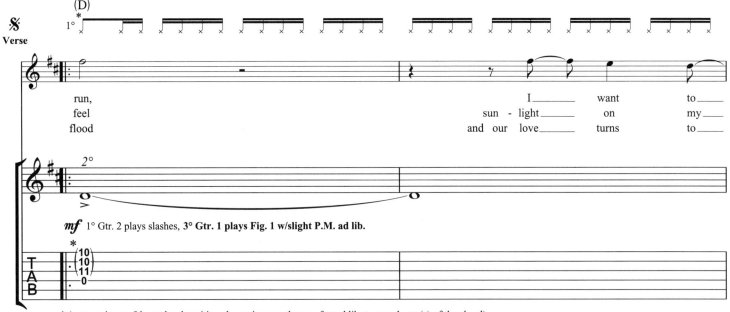

Verse

run,
feel
flood

I_____ want to_____
sun - light_____ on my_____
and our love_____ turns to_____

mf 1° Gtr. 2 plays slashes, **3° Gtr. 1 plays Fig. 1 w/slight P.M. ad lib.**

* (mute strings w/l.h. at chord position shown in parentheses - fret ad lib. to sound note(s) of the chord)

89

—— hide,
—— face.
—— rust.

I —— wan - na tear down —— the walls.
I —— see the dust cloud dis - appear
We're beaten and blown by —— the wind,

let ring - sim.

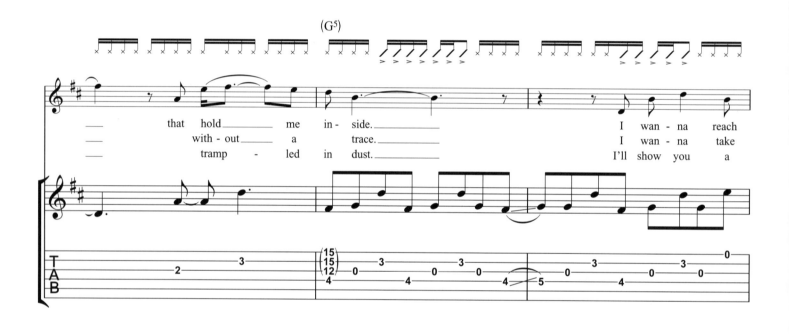

—— that hold —— me in - side.
—— with - out —— a trace.
—— tramp - led in dust.

I wan - na reach
I wan - na take
I'll show you a

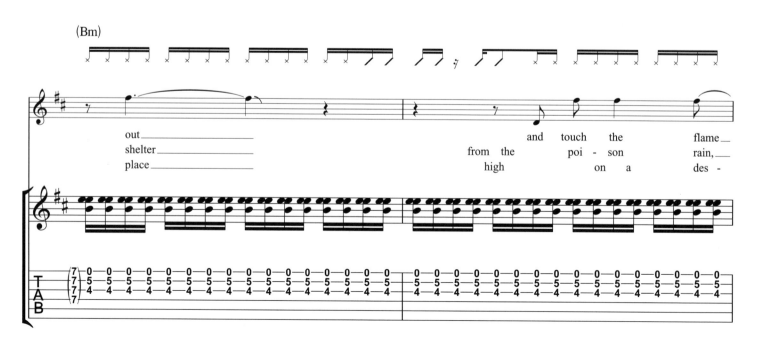

out ——
shelter ——
place ——

and touch the flame ——
from the poi - son rain,
high on a des -

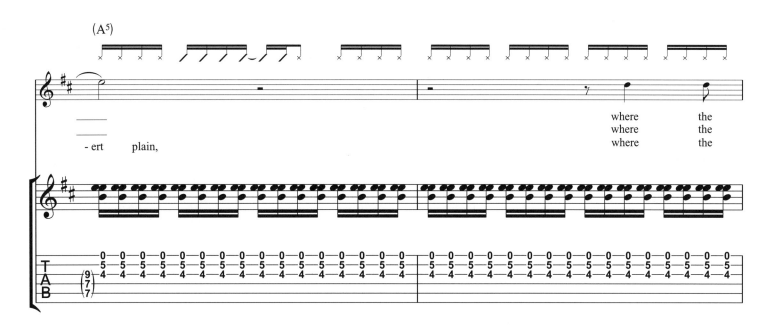

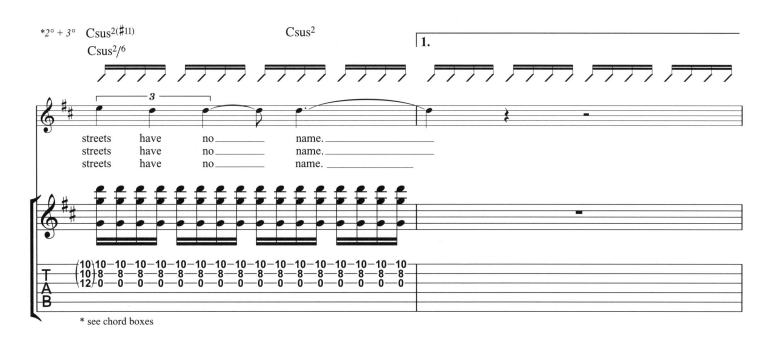

* see chord boxes

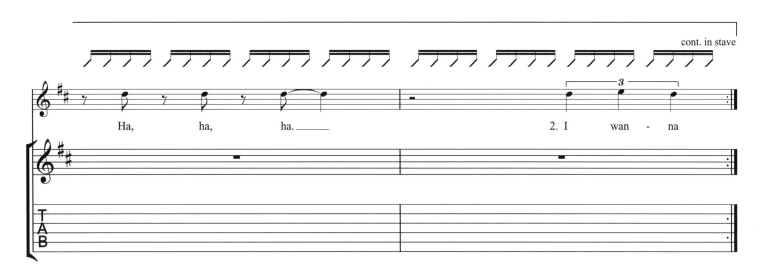

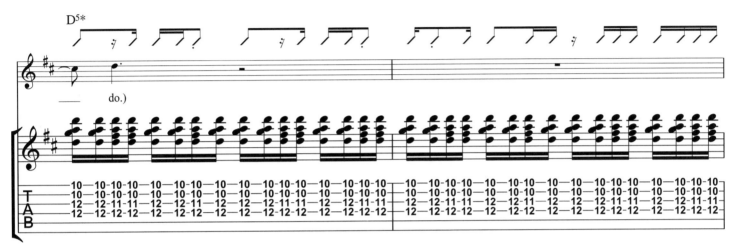

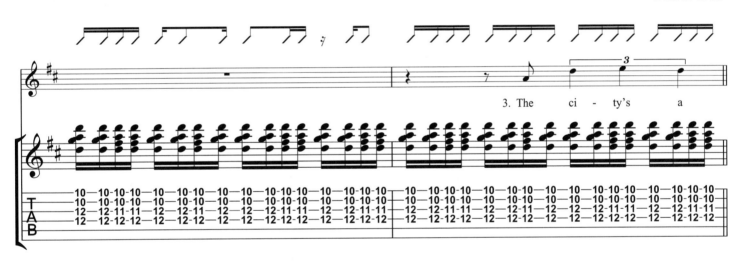

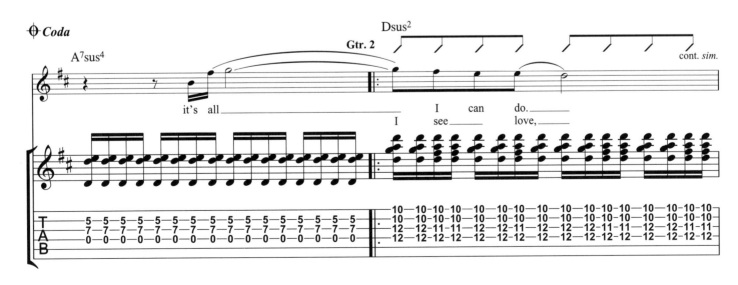

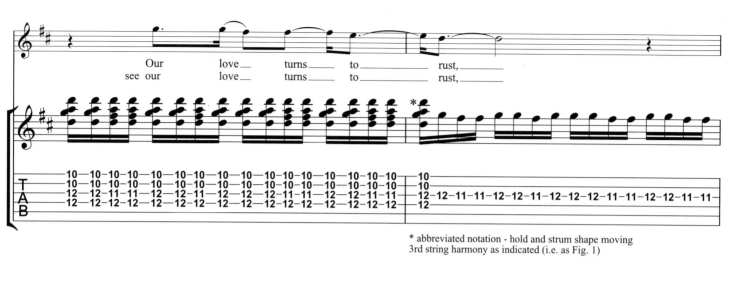

Our love___ turns___ to___ rust,
see our love___ turns___ to___ rust,

```
T 10—10-10-10—10—10-10—10—10—10-10-10—10—10-10-10—10
A 10—10-10-10—10—10-10—10—10—10-10-10—10—10-10-10—10
B 12—12-11-11—12—12-11—12—12—12-11-11—12—12-11-11—12—12-11-11—12—12-11-12—12—12-11-11—12—12-11-11
  12—12-12-12—12—12-12—12—12—12-12-12—12—12-12-12—12
```

* abbreviated notation - hold and strum shape moving
3rd string harmony as indicated (i.e. as Fig. 1)

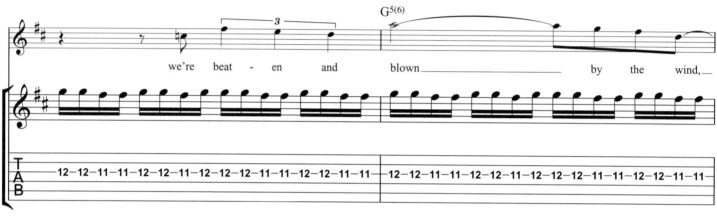

G⁵⁽⁶⁾

we're beat - en and blown___ by the wind,___

```
T 12—12-11-11—12—12-11—12—12—12-11-11—12—12-11-11   12—12-11-11—12—12-11—12—12—12-11-11—12—12-11-11
A
B
```

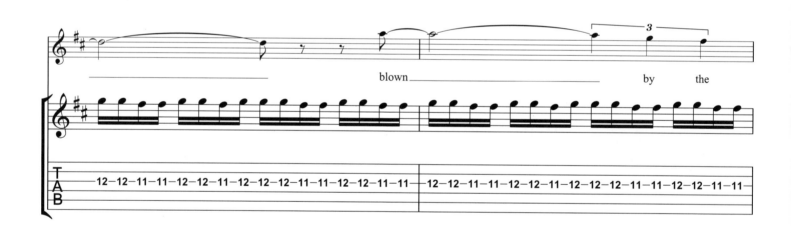

blown___ by the

```
T 12—12-11-11—12—12-11—12—12—12-11-11—12—12-11-11   12—12-11-11—12—12-11—12—12—12-11-11—12—12-11-11
A
B
```

1. wind.   Oh,___   and

2. wind.   Oh___   when I___

```
T 12—12-11-11—12—12-11—12—12—12-11-11—12—12-11-11   12—12-11-11—12—12-11—12—12—12-11-11—12—12-11-11
A
B
```

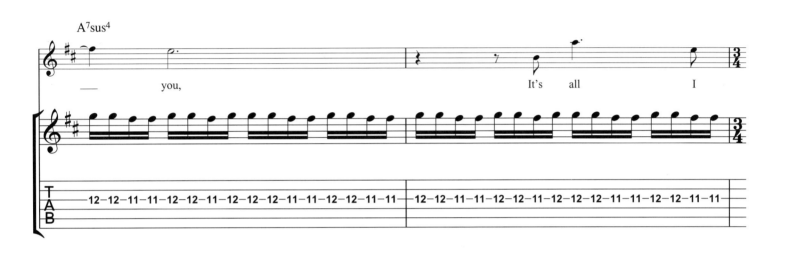

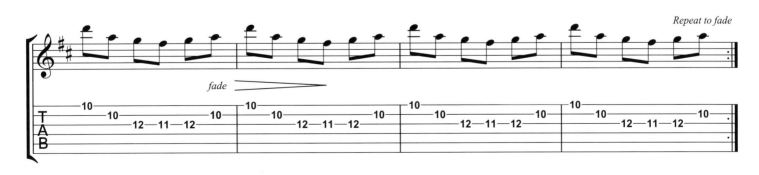

Guitar Tablature Explained

Guitar music can be notated in three different ways: on a musical stave, in tablature, and in rhythm slashes.

RHYTHM SLASHES are written above the stave. Strum chords in the rhythm indicated. Round noteheads indicate single notes.

THE MUSICAL STAVE shows pitches and rhythms and is divided by lines into bars. Pitches are named after the first seven letters of the alphabet.

TABLATURE graphically represents the guitar fingerboard. Each horizontal line represents a string, and each number represents a fret.

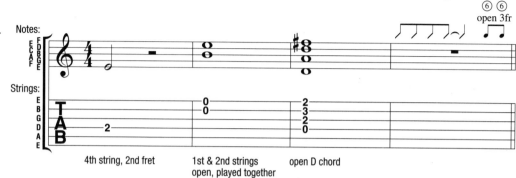

4th string, 2nd fret   1st & 2nd strings open, played together   open D chord

Definitions For Special Guitar Notation

SEMI-TONE BEND: Strike the note and bend up a semi-tone (1/2 step).

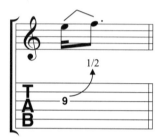

BEND & RELEASE: Strike the note and bend up as indicated, then release back to the original note.

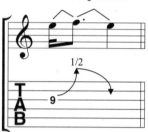

HAMMER-ON: Strike the first note with one finger, then sound the second note (on the same string) with another finger by fretting it without picking.

NATURAL HARMONIC: Strike the note while the fret-hand lightly touches the string directly over the fret indicated.

WHOLE-TONE BEND: Strike the note and bend up a whole-tone (whole step).

COMPOUND BEND & RELEASE: Strike the note and bend up and down in the rhythm indicated.

PULL-OFF: Place both fingers on the notes to be sounded, strike the first note and without picking, pull the finger off to sound the second note.

PICK SCRAPE: The edge of the pick is rubbed down (or up) the string, producing a scratchy sound.

GRACE NOTE BEND: Strike the note and bend as indicated. Play the first note as quickly as possible.

PRE-BEND: Bend the note as indicated, then strike it.

LEGATO SLIDE (GLISS): Strike the first note and then slide the same fret-hand finger up or down to the second note. The second note is not struck.

PALM MUTING: The note is partially muted by the pick hand lightly touching the string(s) just before the bridge.

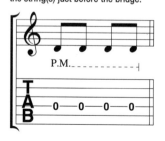

QUARTER-TONE BEND: Strike the note and bend up a 1/4 step.

PRE-BEND & RELEASE: Bend the note as indicated. Strike it and release the note back to the original pitch.

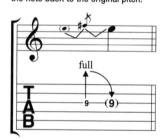

MUFFLED STRINGS: A percussive sound is produced by laying the fret hand across the string(s) without depressing, and striking them with the pick hand.

SHIFT SLIDE (GLISS & RESTRIKE): Same as legato slide, except the second note is struck.

NOTE: The speed of any bend is indicated by the music notation and tempo.

96